An Immigrant's Guide To Success

I0756631

Vol. 1

| *Dream* |

The Story of Lucas

OLAREWAJU OLADIPO, MD. MSc. MBA

Copyright © 2019 Olarewaju Oladipo
All rights reserved. Published by Wundia Books.
Wundia and associated logos are trademarks and/or registered trademarks.
Learn about the author @doctoroladipo on
Facebook/Twitter/Instagram/Pinterest/Google+, and on the
web - **www.olarewajuoladipo.com**

Cover design - Wundia Books.

No part of this publication may be published in whole or in part, or stored in a retrieval system, or transmitted in any form or by any means, electronic, mechanical, photocopying, recording, or otherwise, without written permission of the publisher. For information regarding permission, write to Wundia Books, PO Box 446, Canton MA 02021 USA

First Printing, January 2019

FOREWORD

This book, the first of several books in the series – An Immigrant's Guide To Success, was inspired by a personal journey, one that was not smooth by any means, but a journey that has solidified my belief in the human spirit, and the power that lies in every one of us to achieve whatever goals we set our hearts on. In my experience as an immigrant, starting from the time I left my home country of Nigeria, as a young man with great drive and determination to succeed, I have found that lack of guidance tops the list of the barriers that every immigrant face in their pursuit of a greener pasture in another country. Next to it is lack of knowledge.

Using story-telling as a tool for illustration, the pitfalls that many immigrants face are brought to life in the various books that make up this series. In using this approach, I am challenging your power of imagination, such that you can see yourself in the many stories told in the books in this series. I also believe that you can take that extra step, and borrow from the inspiration of the stories, and use it to energize yourself in the pursuit of your wishes and desires. While the books in this series have been written with the average immigrant in mind, I believe there are life lessons to be learned by anyone who picks up a copy of this book.

It is my sincere hope that you, the reader, irrespective of your age, or your stage in the journey of success will find wisdom in the pages of these books.

DEDICATION

This book is dedicated to all those who through their random acts of kindness, have made it possible for total strangers to fulfill their dreams in a foreign land.

| DREAM |

A Dream For A Season

There is nothing worse than being an immigrant without a dream. It is fascinating to observe how many of us take several months to prepare for the opportunity to immigrate to another country, but when the opportunity finally arrives, fail to make the most of it.

While a good proportion of immigrants know exactly why they have selected a particular country as a destination, and have a clear idea of how to achieve their goal, a good number embark on their journey, only to realize that they had no big ambition with respect to what to do once they arrive at their destination. While successfully immigrating to a new country is a major achievement on its own, and most of the times, driven by a desire, or a dream, it is only the beginning. Successfully immigrating to another country is often the result of a well-executed plan, one that takes a significant amount of planning, sacrifice of self, and sometimes sacrifice on the part of family members. I see immigrating to a new country as the end of one journey, one takes you to the beginning of the next. It is this equally important journey that is the subject of this book, with a major emphasis on having a dream. This latter journey may be the journey of a lifetime, and may determine your future altogether.

Frankly, I believe this second journey is more important than the first, and frequently, it becomes the yardstick by which you may have to measure the outcome of your first journey, or even life's success. In the story that is shared in this book, you will come to appreciate the relevance of this point. It is not unusual for immigrants, especially young ones to mistake their successfully gaining entrance into a country like say, the United States of America, United Kingdom, Australia, or Canada as an end-point in itself, with a considerable number of them losing their original zeal, and the enthusiasm that got them into those countries in the first place. This pattern of behavior, one that can simply be described as a *laisse faire* attitude is not just limited to young adults, it is no respecter of age, and can creep in slowly into the hearts and minds of older adults, irrespective of their level of achievements, or education. In fact, no one is immune to this malady of complacency, although, some are more affected than others. It is much easier to identify this attitude in others, than it is for us to recognize it in ourselves.

In trying to understand why someone would spend their life savings, bear untold hardships, sometimes travel through treacherous terrains, and forgo all they possess to make it to another country, only to make it to that country, and fail to make the most of what the country offers, all you need to do is to look around you. You will easily find one, or two people, and maybe, more that fit into that image. Maybe that person is you, your spouse, or even your children, some who are indirectly connected to your journey. The fact is that anyone of us could easily be affected. For those who see this happening in people around them, it often forces the question – what happened?

For some people, it is quite simple to explain, in the sense that life just became too comfortable. Once they arrive at their chosen destination, they start to take it easy, and let life pleasures get in their way of making progress. In the process wasting their youth, they squander precious moments, and sacrifice their future. For others, it is more complex than that, and as many immigrants can attest, settling in a new country is often an insurmountable task, one that can become overwhelming even to the most prepared of immigrants, forcing them to give in to their circumstances take control, and forget about pursuing any tangible dream.

In this chapter, the aim is simple, that is to set some basic principles, one that can be readily followed, early in your journey, if you are at the beginning, or if you have already immigrated, at any stage of your journey as an immigrant. These principles are never too late to adopt, and can easily fit into anyone's current circumstance. Some of the ideas shared in this guide are based on personal experience, inspiration, observations, and lessons learned from the many immigrants who have made a success of their journeys. Others are based on a wealth of knowledge acquired through an extensive study on the subject of personal growth and self-development. It is the result of the analysis of personal mistakes, and the mistakes of others - friends and acquaintances, who have been generous enough to share the wisdom gained from their experience with me, so that others can all benefit from it.

In the short story that follows the discussion of these guiding principles, you will appreciate the fact that even with one's high level of ambition, and a heart full of big dreams, life in general can be unpredictable, with many dreams shattered along the way. It can be particularly challenging for the unprepared, as there are many variables, some of which are outside of your control.

If you are an immigrant, especially if you have the advantage of age on your side, to embark on your journey without a big dream is like doing yourself a disservice. The aim of this book is to challenge you to dream big, have multiple dreams, and see a bright future for yourself.

Everything Starts With A Dream

Whether you are eighteen when you are about to embark on your journey, or you are sixty-five when your opportunity to immigrate finally arrives, I encourage you to carry out the simple exercise outlined in this section. This is an exercise that can be done at any time, whether you are destined to immigrate, or not, and irrespective of where you stand in your journey. This exercise begins with a simple step, costs little in terms of materials, but requires that you allocate some time - about an hour to two hours of your free time. It is an exercise you must do alone, and one that you should preferably keep to yourself, unless it is absolutely necessary that you share it with your spouse, or whoever you consider to be important in the pursuit of your dream. The great thing about this exercise is that all the steps are relatively simple, except for one, although it is not that tasking.

The first step of this exercise is to buy yourself a small journal. If you don't have a journal, get a small notepad, or any book that can serve a similar purpose. Make sure it is of good quality, preferably with a hard cover, and can withstand wear and tear in the years to come, as you will have to carry it with you for a long time. The journal does not need to be a special purchase, and you can fashion any notepad, or book that you already possess in your household for this purpose. You can fortify the covers – front and back, by reinforcing it with layers of tape, or even attaching a layer of cardboard fixed with glue. Once you have acquired a dedicated journal, or notepad as advised, you can proceed with the next step.

Set a specific time to engage in this exercise. In selecting an ideal time, consider a time of the day when you are least likely to be disturbed, and it does not matter if it is daytime, or nighttime. The less the amount of distraction, the better it is for you, and the more likely it is that you will gain the most from the exercise. Whenever I do this exercise, I do it in the middle of the night, but I understand that not everyone like to stay awake at night. Whatever time of the day you select for this exercise, make sure it is when you are very alert and attentive. Not after a heavy meal, or after completing a long distance travel, or after finishing a long day at work.

Then select a dedicated place to carry out this exercise. In the same way that your choice of time was dictated by a need to avoid any interruption whatsoever, the same applies to your choice of place. For many people, the ideal place may be your home, for others it may be the quiet corner of a café or a coffee shop, although you may not have the luxury of a complete solitude in those places. You may even have to try a location out well before you embark on the exercise to see if it will work for you, or not. The whole idea is that you want to pick a place where no one can easily interrupt your thoughts, a place where you can achieve a reasonable amount of quiet, or if at all possible, complete solitude. If you wonder, why all this preparation for what seems like a mundane and simple exercise, you are not alone. What you are about to do is to engage in one of the most important things you may ever do in your life – it is to write out your dream. In my experience, this very important exercise is engaged in by a minority. The reason is obvious – lack of knowledge, as many people see no sense in it at all, not to talk about dedicating any reasonable amount of time, or effort to it. If you are still wondering about the relevance of this exercise, ask yourself this question – what am I living for? Then think deeply about how you left your home country and the price you had to pay to get to your new country, then ask yourself another question – why am I here? If the answers to these questions comes to you easily, then you do not need this book.

The excuse that many give is that they have it all in their heads. That is a fair excuse if all you have is one dream, but what do you do when have a separate dream for your profession, one for your family, or even one for the community where you find yourself.

You will also see the relevance of this exercise as you read and follow the additional instructions on what to do with what you end up writing in your journal. With all the material steps completed, that is, getting your notebook and your pen ready, and once you have allocated a set time and identified an ideal place, then the core of the exercise begins. I call this journal or notebook the *"dream book'*.

On the first page of the journal, write your full name, your country of destination if you know it, or desired destination if you are yet to accomplish this dream, then note the date when you start making entries into your *'dream book'*. You will notice that all the steps outlined so far, appear mundane, and are just simple instructions. There is a simple reasoning here – in your preparation lies the seeds of your success. This is one of the reasons, I have devoted a little time and effort towards getting you prepared. This approach also helps the psyche, which becomes attuned to the activity you intend to engage in, and activates your brain to be at alert. Even though the basic instructions have been provided, there is absolutely nothing wrong with you developing your own personal routine, or a schedule that works best for you. This is so, because, as you may find out later after completing this exercise for the first time, you may be one of those that turn this practice into a weekly, or monthly activity. So, if that is your preference, please go for it, create your choice of setting, or an ideal environment that works best for you. This is so important because in years to come, after you have discovered the value of this exercise in its entirety, and have begun your journey, you will find yourself going back to your *dream book'*, and repeating the process again and again.

Once you have met the essential requirements as outlined in the last few pages, you can proceed with the task at hand – that is, to begin to write down your dream, or dreams. It is the only part of this exercise that is tasking as it demands a mental input, and requires a degree of focus and introspection. It is also not as easy as it seems, until you actually begin to write. As you begin to write down what you consider to be your dreams, do not over-think the process, but instead, write from the depth of your heart, write about your inner desires, write with sincerity, and write like a dreamer, like someone who truly believe in the power of dreams. Write, until there is nothing else to write about your dreams and aspirations.

Do not be constrained in your writing and let your thoughts flow freely on paper. As you begin to write, you will surprise yourself with what comes out on paper. Write dreams that extend across all the dimension of your life as you would like to see it happen. Write without fear, without self-doubt, and with the mindset that you have nothing to lose. Write until you run out of anything else to write. When you feel that you are done, maybe an hour, two hours, or more, as you may come to find out as a total surprise, then close your *'dream book'*. Do not return to it for at least another twenty-four hours, maybe longer. There is no precise time as to when you should do this, as long as you remember to return to it. I have found twenty-four hours to be optimal, although in my experience, many people cannot wait for the twenty-four hours to quickly pass, so that they can return to read what they had written.

There is a simple reason for this. For many, it is the first time they have had the courage to write down their dreams. Some have not even exercised the thought of having a dream, outside of what we all experience during sleep. Not that they don't have one. Almost every one of us can remember making utterances like, 'my dream job', or 'my dream house'. Occasionally, we may tell someone about our life's dream in conversations, but we may never take it beyond the spoken words of our mouth.

Another reason why many people cannot wait for the twenty-four hours to pass is so that they can return to add more to what they had written. For suddenly, the first exercise has challenged them even further to exercise that part of their mind. It is common to experience this feeling. In fact, for some, soon after they finished putting their thoughts on paper the first time, and as soon as they close the cover on their *'dream book'*, they realize they did not really pour out all their inner desires. The reality is, not many of us can complete this exercise in the real sense at that first seating. With that in mind, feel free to return to your *'dream book'*. Do it as many times as you feel, until you are satisfied. And that is exactly what you should do if that is your situation. But instead of opening you *'dream book'* every hour, wait for some time to pass. In my case, I give myself twenty-four hours to do so.

If you choose to write more and add to what you already wrote, I recommend that you don't read what you wrote earlier at this stage, and try to take your mind off what you had previously written. Instead, relax and be prepared to repeat the same exercise as when you made your first entry. Try as much as possible to do this in a setting similar to what you had the first time when you wrote into your journal. Remember to write the date and time of your entry. When you are done, close the cover of the book, and wait for at least another twenty-four hours before going back to it. If you feel like you still have more to write, repeat the exercise again, and again, each time adding to what you had previously written, and anything else that you had not thought to write about earlier. Remember to write the date and time of your entry. When you are done, close the cover of the book again, and wait for at least another twenty-four hours before returning to your journal. You will observe that every time you return to your journal, you will have less and less to write about. You will soon find yourself at a point when there is absolutely nothing else to add. At that moment, you are ready to move on to the next step.

Even though you have exhausted all the dreams in your head at that point in time, remember that the act of writing down your dream in a journal or a book is not a one-time event, neither is it a final exercise. Not having anything else to add at that moment in time only means that nothing that is significant matter to you at that point in your life. And since what you have written down in your book as your dreams is not a final list, you can always go back and add to your dreams. If you don't already know, you need to understand that a great portion of our dreams will not even show up on the radar of our thoughts, and many times it will be revealed to us as we advance in age. In fact, many of the dreams that we end up documenting in our book will be triggered by a significant event, a memorable circumstance, or a unique life encounter.

In just the same way that the recollection of your desires and dreams for the purpose of documenting them in a journal or a book is not a single event, so is the relevance of your dreams to the different seasons of your life. The majority of your dreams are placed in your hearts to carry you through a season, and many tend to manifest in time for you to be a witness, and enjoy the fruits of your imagination. On the contrary, some dreams will make the substance of a journey of a lifetime, and some may not come to fruition until years later, decades later, or even in one's own lifetime, only to become a part of one's legacy.

The next step of this exercise is one that requires a great deal of attention. There is really no urgency to this stage of the exercise, and it can be done at your leisure. It requires that you painstakingly read through all that you had written down in your 'dream book' from the beginning to the end in one seating. There is also a time requirement to this aspect, as well as a need for a dedicated time and space. Rather than begin to do this on the same day, or night when you made the last entry into your book, I often recommend giving yourself a period of seven days before completing this step. While there is no rhyme or reason why I have selected seven days as a waiting period, I have found it to be about enough time to think through all that you have written.

As you embark on this process, take the time to read through every line of what you had written. As you read through, think of your dreams as a real possibility, and try to imagine yourself in all you have written. As you read through your book, slowly begin the process of committing the essential details to your memory. The first time you read through your *dream book'* may leave you with an unusual feeling, and you may find it outright overwhelming. If that is your experience, take a deep breath. It is a good feeling, and an indication of the depth and breadth of your dream and aspirations. I sometimes feel the same way every time I read the book that contains my list of dreams and aspirations.

After reading through the first time, make an effort to go through it again, this time, doing so at a much slower pace. Don't be surprised if some parts of your dream begin to stand out more than others. You may also surprise yourself to see how grandiose some of your dreams seem when you think about the chances of it becoming a reality. If you feel like reading it again, feel free to do so. This exercise ends with one very important step.

This last step is more important than all the other steps that preceded it, but like the other steps, is very simple. It is to say your prayer. Do so in the best way that you know how to. It does not have to be perfect, as long you identify the dreams you have outlined as the subject of your prayer. End your prayer with the words – *May my dreams come true.* Once you are done saying your prayer, close the cover of your book, and keep it in a safe place. Thereafter, at least once a month, retrieve your *'dream book'* wherever you kept it and read through it. Every time you read through your journal, end the reading session with a prayer, and end it by saying – *May my dreams come true.*

By regularly reading the entries you have made in your journal or book, you are able refresh your memory of you dreams, identify the ones that have been fulfilled, and the ones that are yet to materialize. This routine also serves as reminder to keep your faith, and in ways that cannot be explained, bring the dreams that are yet to be fulfilled into focus and closer to reality. At any point in time, you can always return to your *'dream book'*, make additional entries to add to your dreams, using the steps that were outlined earlier in this book. Remember to date and sign your name after each entry. This practice will soon become an habit. This simple exercise is of immense value and has an inherent power, especially when initiated in the early stages of your planning to immigrate. It can also be applied well after you have immigrated. This exercise has a way of shaping your journey, and in ways that cannot be fully explained by simple logic, may determine your overall success.

The Power Within You

If you are still wondering what the relevance of the described simple exercise is, all you need to do is to think back to when you were a little child. Let your memory take you back to those days when your mind was very open and receptive to the magical influence of the power of imagination. Then ask yourself one simple question. Now that you are an adult, how often do you sit down and imagine things? To take it further, when was the last time you give a thought to what precisely your dreams are? The fact is that within every one of us, there lies that ability to be influenced by the power of imagination. It may have been suppressed, but it never disappeared. What changed as we got older is that we fail to exercise that dimension of ourselves, such that we are limited by our disbelief, and doubt takes hold of our inner thoughts.

As I wrote earlier, everything starts with a dream. Many things that we end up achieving in life, no matter how little, has its foundation in a dream. Though many of us have never cultivated the habit of writing our dreams down, you will be surprised what you will discover if over the years, we have all kept a *dream book*. How does this discussion relate to the journey of an immigrant? To an extent, your success in a foreign country as an immigrant is somewhat influenced by your ability to activate your power of imagination. To dream, is to let your imagination run wild and to freely picture that which you desire for yourself in life. In taking the time to dream, you force yourself to think well into the future, and create an imaginary world of what you want yours to look like, be it your job, your spouse, your children, or your influence on others and the world in general. To let yourself dream, is to take a simple step of faith, and believe that all the different dimensions of your dream has a good chance to become real. It is a simple activity that you can engage in without the need for another participant.

The exercise that was outlined in this book can be readily performed by anyone, yet many people pass on it, and some people see it as a frivolous exercise, and prefer to proceed to the more visible tasks of setting personal goals, making elaborate plans, and going about the business of executing their plans. A good number of people go on to achieve great things without any prior documentation of their dreams. If that person is you, you may already have a winning formula, and you are self-motivated. This group of individuals see their dream as a by-product of the other important steps that they have taken to achieve their goals. There is nothing wrong with this approach, and in many instances may lead you to achieving your chosen dream in record time.

The exercise as described in this book, in which we begin by identifying our dreams allows us to tap into a special power, it is the special power that faith plays in making our dreams come true. By ignoring the significance of faith in this context, many of us go about life thinking that we can achieve all we can simply by our ability to plan, strategize and work hard. We will talk about the importance of faith in the pages that follow. In the short story at the end of this book, you will appreciate the value of having a well-thought out dream, and allowing faith to shape one's course.

Remember that writing down your dream does not mean that you have all the answers at the time you are writing them down, it does not mean that you have any clue on how it will happen, neither does it mean that you possess the ability to bring it into existence at that point in time. It is an exercise that if you wish, you can complete in total secrecy. In fact, there is no need for anyone to be privy to your dream, after all, it is personal to you. It means that you can be as bold as you want, and be as ridiculous as you desire. One requirement that this exercise demands is that you should be true to yourself, and be sure that whatever you note down in your journal or book is what you genuinely desire. Make sure your dreams are such that when they do materialize will give you great joy, delight and a sense of fulfillment.

What Has Faith Got To Do With It

While no one has an answer as to when anyone's dream will come true, it is not uncommon to see the desire of one's heart when backed by unshakeable faith, come into existence over time. None of us have a real understanding of how faith works, especially when it comes to its role in turning dreams into reality. There have been countless instances of such occurrences all over the world, with those affected describing such events as all the dream they ever wished for. To those who do not believe in such occurrences, they see it as a form of mystery for the lack of a better word. For those of the religious faith, it is not that difficult for them to comprehend such a thing happening in their lives, and even becoming a beneficiary of such an event.

In the difficult moments in our lives, when many of us have had to face challenges, we remember having to reach down into our faith, and on many occasions can testify to the victory that followed. For those victories, many of us can deny that our faith had something to do with. It did not mean that you did not back your faith up with hard work, or not having to make necessary sacrifices. When we see ourselves beating the odds, and seeing victories in situations where others have given up, you can always count on your faith playing its role. Faith is what fills the gap between what can be explained through simple logic, and a reality that completely defies logic. It is what is present when all the facts and evidence do not match what manifests in our circumstances. It often explains life events that are so rare, yet it happened to one person, and could not be replicated in another person given the same circumstance. By allowing faith to play its role in the realization of your dream, it means you are willing to rely less on your personal ability, and agree not to depend purely on human intelligence to make your dream a reality.

Faith is the force that you activate when you subject the elements of your dreams to the simple act of prayer. It is the weapon you deploy when you see that what makes up the dreams in your *dream book* is beyond the realm of what you can single-handedly achieve. By letting your faith in on the expression of your dreams, it means you are willing to free yourself of the burden of self-limitation, and surrender to the power of providence, a power that knows how to make something out of nothing, and specializes in the business of making what seems like an impossible dream come into real existence.

With faith, you are able to conquer self-doubt, invigorate your spirit, and gain the confidence to believe in yourself. It enables you to exercise hope and to anticipate a better tomorrow. Whatever your faith, you do your dream a great disservice when you fail to cover it with the power of prayer. No matter how small, or big your dream is, you should never under-estimate its power in the fulfillment of your dream.

Make Your Dream Your Prayer

Reading through your journal at timed interval is a way of familiarizing yourself with your aspirations. When you go back after many months to review some of the things you wrote in the past in your journal or book, you will be surprised how much of it you have forgotten, even for those dreams that have come to fruition. The same can be said of prayers; we often forget what we prayed for, unless we have a way of referring back to it. It is the nature of the human mind, with those things that are no more our priorities constantly displaced by what we believe are currently relevant.

Making your dreams your prayer is simple to understand. Since the last step every time you read the record of your dream is to say the prayer – *'May my dreams come true'*, you in effect turn your dreams into a portion of a prayer. Come to think of it, would you not rather put your dream into your prayer? Would you not rather do so regularly if that is all it takes? If your dream means so much to you, would you not turn it into a prayer, and do so weekly, daily, or even hourly? While it may seem like another routine with no easily understandable basis, I see it as part of a process that contributes in a unique way to the fulfillment of your dream. Once you begin to implement this practice into your routine, you will realize that the more you read through your journal or book, the more you are reminded of all that it contains, the more of it you will commit to memory, and the more you will find it becoming a part of your prayer. It's as simple as that.

As highlighted in earlier paragraphs, since the act of regularly reading your book of dreams is followed by a prayer, your written dream becomes a special prayer. And since prayer has the power to turn what is yet to be into what may come pass, you are further empowering your dream; you are tapping into the spiritual influence that often plays its part in making our dreams become our reality. You may never fully understand how this whole thing works, it not an exact science, nor is it an art, but you will always observe the difference in outcome between those who turn their dreams into a prayer, and those who do not.

Make Your Dream Your Song

This section of the book is important to every one of us but particularly relevant in the case of an immigrant. In making your dream your song, you let it play in your head at all times, and allow it to transform from ordinary words into the lyrics of your heart. It does not really matter if you already immigrated, or whether you are about to embark on your journey. If you are yet to embark on your journey at the time you are reading this book, I recommend that you follow the steps described earlier in this book, and begin writing your dreams down in a journal or a small note pad. Do so if possible, well before you are scheduled to travel, or even well before you purchase your travel ticket.

Irrespective of the state of your journey as an immigrant, or if you are already in your country of destination, remind yourself that you got to the point where you are now because you once had a dream, and that dream was to leave your home country, and to seek a greener pasture in another country. The dream is what set you in motion, forcing you to take all the steps needed to turn a dream into an actual event. The dream led you to set a goal – the goal to travel, the goal then led you to come up with a plan – the plan to obtain become an immigrant, and the plan led to an opportunity – the opportunity of where you are now in your journey. In other words, the dream is what created the opportunity, and everything else in between are the workings of a dream. All the steps you had to take and the struggles you endured were simply there to bridge the gap – the gap between your dream and your reality. In effect, whatever state you are in today, whether you are already set to immigrate, already immigrated, or you have a plan to do so in the future, it is powered by a dream from within, one that was birth by your imagination some time ago. Whichever country you have chosen as your final destination – Ireland, Canada, Australia, United Kingdom, or the United States of America, it only became a choice once you decide to make it your dream.

A dream takes a new meaning when you turn it into a song, it gains a melody of its own, it has a rhythm, a beat, and you become the soloist. The song never stops playing, even when you are asleep. When your dream starts to play in your sleep, it is bound to happen, on the condition that you are willing to play your part, invest your time, devote your energy, and do the work. In making your dream your song, it plays in your head at all times; it becomes your anthem. You will not only sing it when you are alone, you will hum it when it is not convenient to sing aloud. By making your dream your song, you give it power. It's your dream after all, your written words turned into lyrics, and there is no better work of music than the one you have penned yourself. I implore you, whatever your dream is, to make it your song, one that you sing at least once a day, a song that plays in your head day and night, a song that plays in the background while you are working, studying, driving, or while having a shower.

Make Your Dream Your Drink

There is one excuse in my book when someone is allowed to be intoxicated – not with alcohol; it is in the way you let your dream get into your head. There is no stimulant like a powerful dream, it will keep you up at night, keep you focused in the daytime, and always have you energized. Not only will it make the day at hand meaningful, it will give a picture of a future that is worth living for. To be intoxicated with your dream enables you to cope with disappointment, keep failure in perspective, and empowers you to find the gem that is often hidden in those unpleasant outcomes.

Just the way you take a cup of tea, or coffee to stay alert, getting intoxicated with your dream keeps you alert, allowing you to see opportunities that align with your future, and identify avenues to make your dream a reality. The beauty of this approach to handling your dream is that your senses are maintained at all times, and the intoxication only affects your mind. It becomes your weapon against negativity, complacency and self-doubt. It frees you up from the limitations that we pose on ourselves, and blurs the gap between your dream and your reality.

In applying this wisdom to the journey of immigrants, since life in a foreign country is very challenging, to say the least, without a dream that keeps you fired up at all times, you may easily give up and never make real progress. It is the difference between those who arrived on the shore of a foreign country and thrive, and those who get caught in the wave and flounder.

Make Your Dream Your Poster

For many immigrants, making it to a country of their choice is the result of meticulous planning, dogged determination, and singularity of purpose. This step is a significant achievement on its own, and one that is very tempting to consider as an end point in itself. If you talk to many immigrants, some will tell you how while they were still resident in their home country, they had posters of the country they desire to immigrate to all over the walls of their bedroom, or living room. If you ask them why, they all have the same answers. So that they can place the image of where they plan to immigrate to in clear focus, and to keep it within their sight at all times. This seemingly simple action has worked for many people, and continues to work up till today. Whether you paint a picture of your dream on paper and apply it to a wall, or you simply have the texts written on paper and place all around your apartment, it does not matter. All that matters is that you have your dream in clear focus, and within a viewing distance. If you have no walls to paste your poster on, place it on your desk, put it under your pillow, as long as you can see it every day.

What if I Have No Dream

The moment that you think you have no dream often coincides with the moment you realize that it cannot be entirely true. Maybe you have never seen your past achievements as some sort of fulfilled dreams, or maybe you are one of those who go on to do great things without much of a struggle. The issue is not that you do not have a dream, it is possible that you have never considered them to be a dream. It is also possible that your achievements have not been things that you see as unattainable at the time you embarked on them. But dreams do not need to be some extraordinary feat. Once you cultivate the process of writing them down, you soon discover that you have a lot of things yet to be achieved that can be considered a dream in their own rights. A common example is something as important as marriage. Not many people think about it as such a big decision, or something they would consider as a dream, especially in their early years. Some people may consider it worthy of a dream in their late teens, but beyond that age, a lot more people begin to see it as something worthy of being considered a dream. Who wouldn't want to dream about that special person in their future, and how they would like their married life to be. After all, having a dream of meeting a loving and caring person as a life partner will be on top of the list for many of us. If it does not quite fit into a dream yet, for whatever reasons, it would soon become a top dream in the future. Now that you have this example, I am sure that it is easier to see a lot more that is of relevance in your life, things that you can now consider as worthy dreams you would like to write down in your journal or note pad.

All it takes is for you to dare yourself, and search deep within for that deep desire that means so much to you. If no dream in particular comes to mind at the time you begin the exercise of writing things down, do not close your journal for good, instead, over the course of the next few days, think of a desire that if you can achieve it will mean the world to you. In doing this exercise, do not be limited by age, circumstance, or a lack of means or resources to fulfill your dream.

With reference to an immigrant who is already in the country of their destination, all I am encouraging you to do, now that you are in that dream country of yours is to dream beyond just making it there. This exercise is often easier for the young at heart, as they have a buoyant sense of imagination, and they have no problem with letting their imagination run wild. To take the pressure of you, remind yourself that it is only a dream, and it does not have to be precise. No one can judge you by your dream, since no one knows that you have one. So, do not limit yourself in your imagination.

It is also best to write your dream down very early, sometimes even before you begin your journey, when you are not limited in your view of what is possible, or impossible. It is a time when you are yet to be corrupted by others who having failed to make the most of their opportunities, or you are likely to have your enthusiasm dampened by the reality that confronts once you step into that country. All you need to do is to set your mind on your desire to achieve great things in a foreign land. Let your dream be as grandiose as you desire, as long as they are your true desires. You can make your dream as long as you desire. It can be in the form of a letter to yourself, a reminder or a list. You will have opportunities in the future to update your journal and add more to your dreams as time goes on. When you are done writing your dreams down, date it, and sign your name below it. Then move on to the next steps as outlined in the earlier pages of this book.

To Dream Is Only Human

If you have not realized by now, having a dream does not have to be based on pure logic, or common sense. Unlike having a plan, the subject of one of the books in this series, having a dream is not a precise science, or something that relies solely on your understanding, or limited by the extent of your knowledge. For these reasons, you can take that liberty to dare a little, at least more than you would ordinarily do. As you write your dreams down, do not fool yourself thinking you can navigate the way to your dream, relying solely on your intelligence. And since you don't have all the answers, no one person will have all the answers, but together, everyone that shapes your journey will play some role, no matter how minute in making your dream come true.

What is important to know though, is that there is a loose connection between how your dreams turns out, and how much thought you give to thinking about it. The amount of effort you put into thinking and reflecting on your dream has something to do with its achievement. This observation, while it is not based on exact science, is one of the reasons why I recommend letting your dream play a pivotal role, and let it supersede your plan. Having such a mindset means that even when your well-orchestrated plan fails, you will have your dreams to fall back on.

And since your dream is backed by your faith, the two forces work together to ensure that you never give up, and you will be able to persevere in spite of any obstacle you may encounter.

You Can Dream Again

If you talk to many immigrants, you will quickly learn about the disappointments that fill many of their journeys. I have had a good share of mine, and still do, even as I write this book in an effort to ensure that others do a better job of their opportunities and make less mistakes. Dreams may not happen on your time schedule, some of them may not materialize the way you had anticipated them to happen, some dreams may become dashed, but even when these unpleasant outcomes happen, as long as you don't give up, they often lead to another dream.

Disappointment is not unusual for many immigrants, and can happen at all stages of their journey. It may be the case before someone departs their home country, at the immigration entry point, or any time after an immigrant has been in a country of their destination. The unfamiliarity of a new environment, the inherent difficulty of settling down and making a living, and a realization once you are in a new the country that your dream as you wrote it down in your *'dream book'*, is no way close to what is playing out in front of you are all familiar stories. No matter the sentiments that play in your mind, my advice is that you ignore it altogether, and keep your focus.

This feeling of disappointment typical in the early stages of arriving in a foreign country, with many people having gone through it, and many people still going through it. For some, it may last a short period, maybe two weeks, for others it may linger on, and last a few years, especially for those who lack the support of a relative, or an immigrants community. This is where your journal comes in handy; bring it out from where you have kept it, and read through the pages of your journal again, and remind yourself of your dreams.

In the next section of this book, you will read about *'the Story of Lucas'*, a young immigrant who arrived in late winter many years ago to study at a local college in Boston, Massachusetts. In this story, you will appreciate the power of having a dream, the secrets of empowering your dream with your faith, and how every pieces of Lucas' journey became critical pieces of the final puzzle that is the picture of success.

The Story of Lucas

Lucas worked as security officer at a flour mill in the bustling city of Lagos, Nigeria, a job that he settled for after completing his university degree, and after completing a year of national service. With a first-class degree in History, and a desire to pursue a career in academics, he devoted the first two years after completing his university education to applying for positions at various universities within the country. He sent applications far and wide, and he did not mind whatever corner of the country he found a job, as long as it was within the walls of a university. Confident in his ability, he never envisaged the search for such a position will extend over a long time; he thought he would find a position within a year of his completing the year-long national service. Even though he had numerous offers to teach at a number of high schools, he refused to take the offers, hoping for a better opportunity, a job that will set him on a path to becoming an academician and a renowned historian in years to come.

The opportunity that he so desired soon came, but not until almost two years later. In fact, it was at the tail end of the second year of his search. It had the title he so coveted, that of a junior lecturer, although, it was not at his choice of location. He was relieved that he could finally prove all the doubters wrong, many of who thought he was wasting his time, and that he should have accepted the offer of a job at a high school, just like his father. Nevertheless, he was so happy that he could not wait to share the great news with his father; he had lost his mother at the beginning of the first year of his university education. She was his best advocate when she was alive. He had kept the news of the job offer from everyone else, and wanted his father to be the first person to be aware of his success. Since he still lived at home with his father, he waited until later in the evening when his father, who also taught history, would have returned from work.

The job offer was in the northern part of the country. While the pay for the position was not as good as what is offered at the university where he graduated from, he was excited to take the job offer. He was so desperate to take any job, anywhere, as long as it was within the four wall of a university, even with little, or no pay, and provided he has a place to sleep at night, and books to read. He waited at home, restless, and could not wait for his father to arrive, the envelope containing the letter carefully folded in his shirt's pocket. Rather that stay inside the apartment, he sat down on a wooden chair in a balcony to the side of the apartment where they lived on the second floor of a three-story building. Lucas positioned himself such that he could see his father across the street from afar as he approached the house. It was not long after, that he spotted his father walking down the narrow road that led to a side street where they lived.

Excited to meet his father, he ran down a flight of stairs, jumping two steps at a time on the stairs that led to the ground floor of the building. He never made it out to see him in time, as he slipped on the last set of steps and broke his left ankle, with his father meeting him where he lay helplessly, and having to be helped up the stairs. He was later taken to the hospital. All the excitement disappeared in an instant, and instead of him sharing the news of his success with his father, he was writhing in agony from the pain of a broken ankle.

He woke up the following morning at a hospital, with plaster cast on his left leg, and a pair of crutches for company. It was a Saturday morning, and his father was absent when he woke up. He had a bed in a shared room with the other bed next to a window. Later that afternoon, he got up from his bed, got hold of his crutches, and carried himself to the window, standing on one leg at the end of the bed by the window. He freed himself of the crutches and leaned on the ledge of the concrete window frame. He stared through the window into the distance, him mind distant, far away from the small room he found himself in. In his mind played two things, one is the fact that with his left ankle broken, he would not make it to the university where he was offered a position in time to start; the other is the fact that his father had left him a note – to either take a job at the high school, or move out of the house in a month's time. He was lost in thought as he considered his predicament.

A short while later, he returned to his bed, but before he lied down, he lifted his pillow and retrieved the two pieces of paper that were there, one being the letter of a job offer, the other, the note from his father. At that moment, he decided not to tell his father about the offer of the job at the university.

Knowing that there was no way he would make it in time to resume at the university as a junior lecturer, he knew he would have to give up on the only opportunity he had. Tears formed in his eyes as he thought about his situation, looking straight down on the letter, holding it in both hands. He was so engrossed in his own world, that he did not realize someone had entered the room. It was a member of the catering team, an elderly man, in his late sixties.

"Son," he said, tapping lightly on his left shoulder. "What's the matter?"

He was so distraught with what happened that he found solace in sharing his fears with the older man. When he was done narrating all that was on his mind, the man said nothing. Instead, he excused himself, and promised to return in a short while. When he returned, he had in his hands, a tray that contained his lunch – a bowl of brown rice, sautéed spinach and sundried tilapia fish. "I have brought you an extra portion of fish. You know they are expensive." the elderly man said, after setting the tray on a wooden table next to his bed.

Before he departed, he dug into his pants rear pocket and brought out a small, square book about two and a half inches wide. He then knelt on one knee to explain what the book is all about, whispering, as if he did not want anyone else to know what he was talking about. "This small book is called a 'dream book," he said. Before you go to bed tonight, write all the great things you desire for your future. Then close it, say your prayer, and do not open it until you leave this hospital."

Without asking any questions, Lucas collected the book, thanked the man, and placed it under his pillow. The man disappeared soon after, and Lucas settled to eat his meal. Lucas saw the man that one time, and never saw him again until he was discharged from the hospital. He complied with the instructions given to him, and he never opened the book throughout the time he was at the hospital. Once he returned home, he kept the dream book, the letter of a job offer from the university, and the note written by his father in a small compartment in a medium size suitcase. He forgot about the book altogether while he got busy making plans to vacate the apartment he shared with his father. As part of his plan, Lucas decided to leave the rural part of the country where his father lived and moved to the urban city of Lagos. He secured his job as a security officer in the second week of arriving in the city.

Having suffered the misfortune of losing his mother a few years earlier, and the accidental injury during which he broke his left ankle, Lucas wondered what life has in store for him, and could not understand why he was beset with such misfortune. Even though his work as a security officer paid more than he was been offered at the university where he was offered a position, he was not particularly pleased with the direction of his career. All day, he works behind a glass shield, studying a number of cameras, and watching the trucks that come and go through the gates of the flour mill. Seven months into his job as a security officer, he was involved in foiling an attempt to steal a truck load of wheat flour from one of the warehouses, to which he alerted the police in a timely manner.

Even though he got personal recognition for doing a great job, and for stopping what could have been a major loss at the factory, he did not see his role as anything extraordinary. That same day, on the way home, he made a mental note to read his dream book when he gets home. With the door of his room locked in the shared apartment that he lived in, he opened his suitcase, retrieved the dream book and began to read what he had written many months ago. While he was fascinated with the extent of what he had written, many of which he had forgotten, one thing stood out, that is not to give up his dream to become renowned academician in a major university. He said a silent prayer and returned the book into the compartment when he got it earlier, and locked the suitcase. On his way to work the following morning, just before he stepped into the small cubicle fitted with different security cameras, he was stopped at the door, by a middle aged woman. "I heard about what you did yesterday. I am very proud of you." At first, he ignored her, walking past her, and he was about to close the door, when the woman announced who she was.

"I own this factory the woman announced." Lost for words, Lucas paused in the small opening left in the half-closed door, his right hand on the door handle"

"At 1.00 o'clock this afternoon, I will send my assistant to get you for a brief meeting in my office," said the woman, before she walked away. When no one sent for Lucas that afternoon, he saw no issue at all, and thought the meeting was so that management can express their gratitude. The meeting eventually took place, but not until a week later, not in the woman's office, but right there in the cubicle where he worked.

"I completed my undergraduate education in the same department that you graduated from. I see that you were taught by one of my old professors at the university," the woman said, at the start of their conversation.

"That must have been some time ago, I believe," Lucas replied, for lack of nothing to say.

"I read through your resume and found out you performed brilliantly in your studies at the university."

"Thank you, ma."

"Is that truly your resume? I don't believe you belong here," the woman said, sending Lucas into a state of panic.

"I love my job, ma. I hope you won't fire me."

"You won't be fired. I know you love your job, but I want you to be sincere with me."

It was only then that Lucas loosened up, and narrated his experience since the time he completed his university education. He talked about the premature loss of his mother, the sour relationship between him and his father over his ambition plans, and his desire to be one of the best in his field. The woman listened attentively, said nothing, until Lucas was done telling his story.

"Your dream is to become an academic historian. Is that right?"

"Yes," Lucas replied, timidly.

"I agree with you. I truly believe you can," the woman replied. Many years ago, I completed my postgraduate studies in Boston, and I believe it is still possible to contact one or two of my professors at the university. I haven't visited in seven years."

"Do you know how much I earn?" Lucas asked, thinking about the cost of an opportunity to acquire such a great education.

"You don't need to tell me," the woman said, curtly.

It would be two years later before the conversation that Lucas had with the woman who owned the factory bore fruits, when during one of the woman's travel to the United States, she obtained an application form for Lucas to apply for postgraduate studies at Boston University, with the flour mill offering a scholarship that covered the full cost of his study and all related expenses.

Lucas went on to complete his PhD in

African History, and winning multiple awards. It was at the same university that he met his wife – who he had previously imagined and documented in his dream book a year earlier. Over the years that followed, Lucas continued to fill the pages of his dream book with more of his personal dreams, and the rest of the pages with dreams he has for his wife, children, and his yet to be born grandchildren.

ABOUT THE AUTHOR

Olarewaju Oladipo is an author (fiction and non-fiction) whose writing career began while practicing as an orthopedic surgeon. Following the release of his earlier books "The White Coat" (2006) and "House Calls" (2007), he dedicated the next few years to crafting motivational quotes written using the Twitter handle @3SqMeals as Dr. O' and publishing multiple books under the '3SqMeals Tweets – Not Your Typical Meal' series.

Using the experience of the challenges he faced earlier in his career, he has channeled his energy into mentoring young international medical graduates in pursuit of advanced education in the Europe and North America, with the establishment of an organizing named, KAINJI. This work later became the foundation of his current engagement in personal development, professional coaching, and public speaking.

His works of fiction include the "North Main Street" mystery series and the "Once A Doc" medical fiction series, with the release of Barber's Haven (2015), 'A Patient called Emma' (2015) and 'Ghost Bus (2016).

'The Sculpture Garden' series is based on actual sculptures and part of an ongoing effort to support the work of local artists in Nigeria, fund the establishment of sustainable sculpture gardens, and sponsor worldwide collaborations with art institutions. Two Blind Men (2017) was the first of a collection of short stories of the 'Sculpture Garden' series. Tortoise of Many Colors (2017), The Tree of Wonder (2017), and Esther (2018) are other books in the series.

All books are available in paperbacks and eBook formats on Amazon, Kobo, Smashwords, and on author's website (**www.olarewajuoladipo.com**).

54

www.ingramcontent.com/pod-product-compliance
Lightning Source LLC
Chambersburg PA
CBHW031919270726
48655CB00006BA/2827